Runes

James K. Baxter

Runes

LONDON
OXFORD UNIVERSITY PRESS
New York   Wellington

1973

Oxford University Press, Ely House, London W.1

GLASGOW NEW YORK TORONTO MELBOURNE WELLINGTON
CAPE TOWN IBADAN NAIROBI DAR ES SALAAM LUSAKA ADDIS ABABA
DELHI BOMBAY CALCUTTA MADRAS KARACHI LAHORE DACCA
KUALA LUMPUR SINGAPORE HONG KONG TOKYO

ISBN 0 19 211828 5

© Oxford University Press 1973

PRINTED IN GREAT BRITAIN BY
THE BOWERING PRESS PLYMOUTH

CONTENTS

ACKNOWLEDGEMENTS

Acknowledgements should be made to the editors of the following journals, in which some of these poems first appeared: *Landfall* and the *Malahat Review*. The poem 'Letter from the Mountains' first appeared in *Frontiers* under the title 'High Country Letter'. The sequence of 'Words to Lay a Strong Ghost' is a revised and extended version of a sequence originally published in *Stand* under the title 'Seven Masks of Pyrrha'.

WORDS TO LAY A STRONG GHOST
after Catullus

THE PARTY

A kind of cave—still on the brandy,
And coming in from outside,
I didn't like it—the room like a tunnel
And everybody gassing in chairs—

Or count on finding you there, smiling
Like a stone Diana at
Egnatius' horse-laugh—not my business exactly
That he cleans his teeth with AJAX,

But he's the ugliest South Island con man
Who ever beat up a cripple . . .
Maleesh—the booze rolls back, madam;
I'm stuck here in the void

Looking at my journey's end—
Two breasts like towers—the same face
That brought Troy crashing
Down like a chicken coop—black wood and flames!

THE PEACH TREE

Pleasant enough to lie
In my friend Allius' condemned house
On a spring Saturday
With a peach tree out in the yard

And a first-rate view of the back of the Oban,
Fire escapes and pipes—
Man, I'm way out!
The big mattress on the floor

And a little brandy,
With Pyrrha's long legs
Under the blanket—the bug-eyed snoopers
Can't make it;

Their radar won't work
In a house more than fifty years old,
Most of all when the staircase
Flutters with tapa mats!

Thanks to Allius
I'm in the saddle now
Riding the tornado—it could break the wings
Right off my glider,

But Pyrrha doesn't talk;
She knows love inside out—I've christened her
Queen of the spring thunder!
It would be good to die

Now—the peach tree will drop its flowers
Today or tomorrow—after the light
Goes out, lady, we're going to have
A long, long sleep.

THE BUDGIE

Pyrrha's bright budgie who would say,
'Pretty fellow! Pretty fellow!'
For bits of cake from her hand is now
Silent in the underworld.

We buried him beside the rhubarb
Ceremoniously in a box
That once held winklepickers—Death,
You've got a hard gullet!

Pyrrha's eyes are red—partly on account of
The bird, and partly for herself,
Because nothing desired can last for long—
That's why she's crying.

THE HYMEN

Virgins!—Callimachus praises
The girl who opens to her man's prick
(Only after the proper contract)
In a motel, or a caravan

Beside the Deep Stream—I don't
Ask that of you, Pyrrha,
To bind or be bound,
Because it's not your style—

If eighteen men climbed up your bush track before me,
Well, I'm the lucky nineteenth!
Cabbages no doubt are virgins
Growing plump behind the wire netting

In each suburban garden, waiting for
The slug to climb and rape them—
You never had another man,
Nor this one either! I camp like old Brunner

Eating fresh water
Mussels boiled with roots of raupo,
At the edge of the impenetrable hymen
Only the dead have broken.

THE EARTH

Pyrrha, as when I lie and cannot
Sleep—the thought of your body
Sets me in mind of the white
Cataract or goddess

Leaping two thousand feet from Lake Quill
Down to the green womb
Of the bush below—
Or else, Mount Iron, when the air shakes

With heat above the rocks and matagouri
In a trance at noonday when the hawk kills—
So you have become a world
Or else the world has narrowed down to you,

Peculiar bondage! I'd forget all this
If in the night you came to me
By your own will, to lay
Your black hair on my pillow,

Your body in the bed beside me,
Cataract or lioness—
I am divided from the earth
Nine days now—nine days of death!

THE CHANGE-OVER

Four times tonight I've heard the bed creaking—
The wall is thinner than cardboard
Or else you don't care! Tears like booze
Are running into my mouth—

He'll find out what it's like! That mug!
It doesn't help me, Pyrrha;
I'm hooked for life—mad enough to think
The sun rose up the sky out of your cunt—

I'm freezing! All the trees have died.
Your mini-skirt sticks to his bed-rail,
And he's the noonday sun. He looks down on
A rough sea of storm-black curls;

One day he'll drown. He'll hang, like me,
An old coat on your clothesline
Pegged up to dry! Better not ever to be
Born than be your man.

THE COUNTER-LUNCH

Nobody gets a look in
When Caelius cleans up the counter-lunch
(They call him Garbage Guts)—
Cheese, chicken, saveloys, black pudding,

It all goes down the hatch—old men get knocked
In the ribs with an elbow-jolt,
And he blows whisky through his red moustache
And tells that boring story

About the moll with rice grains in her fanny—
I'm sorry; I forgot
You love him, Pyrrha—
Well, that's only natural!

If he can do it four times in a night
Other men don't count—but when, my girl,
You grip him in bed
As the vine grips the rock,

Remember it's much the same whether
You kiss his mouth or his arse—the same
Dull buttock-face, the same shitty breath,
The same red tuft of hair.

THE WOUND

It is not women only
Who lose themselves in the wound of love—
When Attis ruled by Cybele
Tore out his sex with a flint knife,

He became a girl. Blood fell
In flecks on the black forest soil—
So it was for me, Pyrrha,
And the wound will ache, aches now,

Though I hear the flute-players
And the rattling drum. To live in
Exile from the earth I came from,
Pub, bed, table, a fire of hot bluegum,

The boys in the bathing sheds playing cards—
It's hard to live on Mount Ida
Where frost bites the flesh
And the sun stabs at the roots of trees,

No longer a man—Ah! don't let
Your lion growl and run against me,
Cybele's daughter—I accept
Hard bondage, harder song!

THE RIVAL

Young Caelius counts himself lucky
To have and hold your body—
He's just begun! How will you like it, Pyrrha,
When he can't raise a stand

But lies beside you in the dark
Boozed up, hating your cold heart
And what's below it, the eight-headed
Sea-rock-monster barking between your thighs?

THE FRIEND

As those cold waters rise at Rainbow Springs
Endlessly from the underworld
(So deep a fountain that the divers cannot
Find its beginning in the groins of earth;

So strong a current that the coins they drop
Spin sideways onto ledges)—
As those fish-breeding waters flow
Under tidy bridges

Bringing some peace to the time-sick traveller—
Your friendship, Allius,
Has lifted for a half day from me
The manacles of Cybele.

THE STREETLIGHT

If they were to put your body in a sack
And dump it in the harbour, weighted down
With iron, for the crabs to feed on—
Or if, using a scoop

And concrete mixer, they put it ten feet under
The centre of the Octagon
(Where, this winter afternoon,
The streetlights burn, and I

Keep your smell in my nostrils,
Your touch like a net of wires
Under my skin)—when you are buried, Pyrrha,
Your flesh will never putrefy—

It takes a stake driven through the heart
To finish off your kind—
The dead can't die!
You prowl in the empty street

Teaching me the self is a mirror
By which the dead come back—I'd like to
Crack the seance, Pyrrha,
With a great fart—it can't be done

That easily! I hate
And love; I love and hate . . .
Under the streetlight it's your mouth that's wet with
    blood:
I'm your refrigerated meat!

THE ROCK

Arms of Promethean rock
Thrust out on either
Side of a bare white strip
Of wave-ridged sand—long before

I ever met you, Pyrrha,
The free world held me in its heart,
And half my grief is only
The grief of a child torn from the breast

Who remembers—who cannot forget
The shielding arms of a father,
Maybe Poseidon—out there
Where the waves never cease to break

In the calmest weather, there's a hump-backed
Jut of reef—we called it Lion Rock—
Growling with its wild white mane
As if it told us even then

Death is the one door out of the labyrinth!
Not your fault—to love, hate, die,
Is natural—as under quick sand-grains
The broken bladders lie.

THE FLOWER

They've bricked up the arch, Pyrrha,
That used to lead into
Your flat on Castle Street—Lord, how
I'd pound the kerb for hours,

Turning this way and that
Outside it, like a hooked fish
Wanting the bait but not the barb—
Or else a magnetized needle!

Well; they've bricked it up—fair
Enough! You've sunk your roots in Australia,
And I'm free to write verses,
Grow old, be married, watch my children clutter

Their lives up. . . . It was always a tomb,
That place of yours! I didn't know
Then how short life is—how few
The ones who really touch us

Right at the quick—I'm a successful
Man of letters, Pyrrha—
Utterly stupid!—a forty-year-old baby
Crying out for a lost nurse

Who never cared much. The principle
That should have made me tick went early
Half underground, as at the paddock's edge
You'll see in autumn some flower

(Let's say a dandelion)
Go under the farmer's boots
Like a faded sun
Cut with a spade.

AT THE GRAVE OF A WAR HERO

One fat nut from the macrocarpa tree
That grows above the garage
Where you kept your bike and rabbit traps—
I plant it at the edge of your military

Slab—*not* as a bribe to Deathwish Drang,
The zombie in charge of this cemetery—
But in hopes it might reach down to Hell
And split the rock and let some light in,

Or that your blind deaf soul may touch it
And smile to remember home—
That endless hangover you tried to wash away
By swimming the Taieri in winter!

You're out of touch, mate—no gear to fiddle—
Nobody to fuck, punch, kick a ball at—
All that self-loving vigour
Swallowed up in Caesar's black mad eye

That imitates Zeus! Yet from here
Death looks to me like the only love affair
Worth having—you rot
In khaki; I in civvies—

Let's say they cut off the toes,
Then the fingers, then the legs at the knees,
Then the hands, then the legs at the thighs,
Then the arms at the shoulders—

Wisdom is this armless legless stump
Howling for its mother! Well, brother,
The War Graves Commission
Has put you in your place

Right where you started from,
Perfectly adjusted, normalized,
In your concrete cabin—till the last flag drops,
Good luck, mate; goodbye!

Within that land there is a range,
And on that range there is a cone,
And on that cone there is a rock,
And in that rock there is a cave,
And in that cave there is a stone,
And on that stone I carved a name,

And the cut letters will remain
At length when there are no more men
But only a little dust fallen
On gully, rock and cone.

AFTERNOON WALK

Along the bank of the Leith the five of us
Were walking that Sunday—first, Bubba
Trundled by Jean in his pushchair—then, you
In your brown slacks, John and I,

Each in his own afternoon—when we came up to
The bridge with its gate and chain, I thought
That the weirs were passionate almost beyond bearing,
That the wind swinging on ropes of willow

Over the water, was not sad at all,
But a voice or a breath from fields of high summer
Where harvesters were sweating—I could all but see
Their foreheads glisten, their back muscles tighten,

In the approval of the wind that washed
Equally over garden and gravestone
And our dry faces. Further on, a wet black dog
Came out of the duckpond shaking himself,

And in the Botanical House everything was green
Except for the turtle resting on a pipe,
His head just out of water—
My brother!—moving his flippers very gently,

Breathing slowly, avoiding any clash
With the enormous leaves of the banana palm
Above him, or the quick small fish below him
Darting over the mud—oh these afternoons

Dedicated to a neurasthenic God
Are hardly his or mine! If, later, when we settled
Down on the concrete rim of a dried-up pond,
And Bubba sat like a Buddha in the sandpit,

I lay down flat and rested, letting others talk,
While the wind kept moving in the macrocarpa
And the red galah birds were screeching
In wire cages—it was not to embarrass

Anybody—it was perhaps to make sure
My own heart was still beating
Stroke on stroke—because, as you know, my dear,
The world has to balance on a turtle's back.

DAUGHTER

Daughter, when you were five
I was your Monster;
Leaving the pub, less than half-alive,
Hurtling in a taxi to the Play Centre—

You'd ride like a jockey up Messines Road,
Thumbs in my eyes, your bulky legs
On each side of my booze-filled head—
A red-suited penguin!

I'd spoon you out dollops of mushroom soup,
Peel off the penguin skin, and tuck you down,
Uncap a bottle of White Horse, dredge up
My hangman cobbers from the town. . . .

Five years later I'd wake at 2 a.m.
And see an upright ghost in a nightie
Standing beside my bed, mumbling
About a bad dream it had had—

You'd settle in with me like a bear cub
And wrap your arms halfway round my chest—
An atomic blast set off in the Sahara
Of my schizoid, never-quiet mind!

Incest? The quacks don't know their job.
I was your father,
I treated you like bone china,
Sent you sleepwalking back to your cot.

At seventeen your face is powder-white,
Your hair is a black dyed fountain,
Mooching round the house you slam doors
And wait to be rung up.

Why won't you work? That boil on your heel
Comes from going barefoot
In the wet streets. Last night
I dreamt I burnt a fish-skin coat

To turn you back into a human shape—
Wouldn't you yell! Yet I was glad
When you hoisted your private flag
Against the bourgeois gastanks—You're *my* daughter!

When I go in to wake you up
On a morning of ice and boredom,
You sleep with your mouth open
Like a soldier struck down in battle,

And I'm Narcissus bending over
The water face! From the edge of the pillow,
Red-veined, grape-black,
My own eye looks back.

MIDWINTER MOON
for Rowley Habib

Rowley, when we met in Princes Street,
You were sick of the Public Works Department,
I was sick of the whole town of ghosts—
It did me good to see
Your beat-up gloomy stubbled Maori face
Coming alive from its own centre—

The cold was a new, difficult dimension;
The cold was an oil-drum with the bottom knocked out;
The cold was strychnine in my veins!

That night I saw the moon like a bullock's skull
Hanging on the scrub fence of Mount Cargill—
I drove the Public Service Garage Holden
Howling up the motorway,
Ten bottles of freezing coke on the seat beside me,
You and your girlfriend in the back.

Harpooned in my seat by the cold, I said to the moon,
Not letting you or your girlfriend hear—
'Midwinter moon, great demon,
Suck out my heart; give me yours!
Take my face of bone and skin;
Give me the face of bare shattered rock
With which you look down on the snakepit of life
Without an atom of pain!'

TO MY FATHER IN SPRING

Father, the fishermen go
down to the rocks at twilight
when earth in the undertow

of silence is drowning, yet
they tread the bladdered weedbeds
as if death and life were but

the variation of tides—
while you in your garden shift
carefully the broken sods

to prop the daffodils left
after spring hail. You carry
a kerosene tin of soft

bread and mutton bones to the
jumping hens that lay their eggs
under the bushes slily—

not always firm on your legs
at eighty-four. Well, father,
in a world of bombs and drugs

you charm me still—no other
man is quite like you! That smile
like a low sun on water

tells of a cross to come. Shall
I eavesdrop when Job cries out
to the Rock of Israel?

No; but mourn the fishing net
hung up to dry, and walk with
you the short track to the gate

where crocuses lift the earth.

MOTHER AND SON

I

Blowflies dive-bomb the sitting-room
Table, this dry spring morning,

In my mother's house. As I did in my 'teens,
I listen again to the Roman-lettered clock

Chiming beside the statue of Ghandi
Striding towards God without any shadow

Along the mantelpiece. Time is a spokeless wheel.
Fantails have built a nest on the warm house wall

Among the passion vines. The male one lurks.
The female spreads her fan. Out in the rock garden

White-headed my mother weeds red polyanthus,
Anemone, andean crocus,

And the gold and pearl trumpets called angels' tears.
Mother, I can't ever wholly belong

In your world. What if the dancing fantail
Should hatch tomorrow a dragon's egg?

Mother, in all our truces of the heart
I hear the pearl-white angels musically weeping.

2

There's more to it. Those wood-framed photographs
Also beside the clock, contain your doubtful angels,

My brother with hair diagonally brushed
Over his forehead, with a hot dark eye,

And myself, the baby blondish drowsing child
So very slow to move away from the womb!

Saddled and ridden to Iceland and back by the night-
    hag
He learnt early that prayers don't work, or work

After the need has gone. Mother, your son
Had gained a pass degree in Demonology

Before he was twelve—how else can you make a poet?—
Yet we're at one in the Catholic Church.

I go out to meet you. Someone is burning weeds
Next door. The mother fantail flutters

Chirping with white eyebrows and white throat
On a branch of lawsoniana, and the darting

Father bird comes close when I whisper to him
With a susurrus of the tongue.

AT RAKIURA

You may be sure no matron will ever row out
To get a child by sitting on the snouted rock

At the centre of the harbour. That phallic monster is
Of danger only to the seaplane

Taxi-ing in past the wooden lighthouse
Where muttonbirds sqawk in their burrows

Growing fat for the Maori. No mitigation
Of the sense of being trapped by life

Will come to us from the shelves of the museum
Where they've stacked the junk of the early days,

Bullets, clay pipes, paper money,
The Lord's Prayer written on a seashell.

But honeymooners may sponge out a quarrel
With a kiss that gathers half its meaning

From beaches where the surf bangs over
Like the cracking of a two-mile-long flax whip,

And we who are older look at the headstones of
The grim dead, as ignorant as ourselves,

Those whom the cold Strait or whisky killed,
And go back to the guesthouse to stretch out

And hear the chug of a generator
Or the monotonous rumble of the wind above

The high roof, not talking, just lying
And thinking of nothing on a sagging bed

That would extend (I imagine) an equal tolerance
To a paying guest or a moneyless suicide.

AT THE FRANZ JOSEF GLACIER

The hot rust-coloured springs in the riverbed
Were dry, but a smell of sulphur

Haunted the trees along the faultline
Under the glacier face where the guide

Split with his ice axe a boulder of cunninghamite
And showed us the small rock garnets

Like blood drops. Brunner wrote of this country:
'March is a bad month to ford the rivers

On account of the moss that grows . . .' Yes, explorer,
Deerstalker, have to pass the needle's eye

To get where they are going. The griefs I carry
Are nothing. All men die. What sign

Can I leave on cairn or tree to tell
The next comer that my thoughts were human?

As red moss grows on the glacial stone,
Then thicker spores whose acid crumbles it

A little—then the seeds the birds may drop,
Making their own earth, sending down roots,

Cracking and rending the rock—so may my words
Give shade in a land that lacks a human heart.

AT THE FOX GLACIER HOTEL

One kind of love, a Tourist Bureau print
Of the Alps reflected in Lake Matheson

(Turned upside down it would look the same)
Smiles in the dining room, a lovely mirror

For any middle-aged Narcissus to drown in—
I'm peculiar; I don't want to fall upwards

Into the sky! Now, as the red-eyed tough
West Coast beer-drinkers climb into their trucks

And roar off between colonnades
Of mossed rimu, I sit for a while in the lounge

In front of a fire of end planks
And wait for bedtime with my wife and son,

Thinking about the huge ice torrent moving
Over bluffs and bowls of rock (some other

Kind of love) at the top of the valley—
How it might crack our public looking-glass

If it came down to us, jumping
A century in twenty minutes,

So that we saw, out of the same window
Upstairs where my underpants are hanging to dry,

Suddenly—no, not ourselves
Reflected, or a yellow petrol hoarding,

But the other love, yearning over our roofs
Black pinnacles and fangs of toppling ice.

AT KURI BUSH

A few days back I climbed the mound
Where the farmhouse had stood,

As green as any that the Maoris made
Along that coast. The fog was blowing

Through gates and up gullies
Hiding even the stems of cocksfoot grass

That had sprung up in place of
The sitting-room table and the small brass

Kerosene lamp my mother lighted
Every night, whose white wick would burn

Without changing colour. Somebody must have
Used the old brushwood fence for kindling

Twenty years ago. Outside it
My father stood when I was three or less,

Holding me up to look at
The gigantic rotating wheel of the stars

Whose time isn't ours. The mound yielded
No bones, no coins, but only

A chip of the fallen chimney
I put in the pocket of a damp coat

Before I bumbled back down to the road
With soaking trousers. That splinter of slate

Rubbed by keys and cloth like an amulet
Would hold me back if I tried to leave this island

For the streets of London or New York.
I hope one day they'll plant me in

The kind of hole they dig for horses
Under a hilltop cabbage tree

Not too far from the river that goes
Southwards to the always talking sea.

THE COMMUNIST SPEAKS

Do not imagine I could not have lived
For wine, love or poetry,
Like the rich in their high houses
Walking on terraces above the sea.

But my heart was caught in a net
Woven out of strands of iron
By the bleak one, the thin one, the basket-ribbed
Coolie and rickshaw boy

Who has not learnt the songs that ladies like,
Whose drink is rusty water,
Whose cheek must rest on a dirty stone,
In whose hands lie the cities of the future.

WINTER RIVER

Nothing is colder than this water in winter
when winds crack the lopped pines
on the domain bank and send cones
rolling down to the water . . .

Thick bare brown roots tangled
below the sod wall. The boys
and their girls would sit on Saturdays
in a fog of awkwardness and watch

the river run out to the bay.
Ah well—it's easy
to come back, more or less alive
inside one's own unbreakable

glass dome, a dying Martian,
and think about youth.
I never liked it much.
I did not venture

to touch the thick blonde matted curls
of those man-swallowing dolls, our big sisters.
I had no sister.
Their giggles made me tremble

and coast away to the bathing shed latrine
in itchy summer torpor,
furiously inventing a unicorn
who hated the metal of Venus.

Yet they weren't metal. Now
they sag on porches, in back rooms,
flabby as I am, and the river
carries a freight of floating pine cones.

IRON SCYTHE SONG

An appearance of control
Is what the waves could drown;
Seawater like the soul
Is ownable by no one
Though safe enough to watch,
And as I barge through each

White haggard tumbling top
The cold surf bangs my head,
And quickly I go up
To change in the bathing shed,
Leaving my wife and son
To plunge alone,

Then fat and fortyish
With a king-sized ice cream
Snug in its cone, I splash
Through the warm creek and come
Up the road's stony edge
To my father's hawthorn hedge . . .

'The scarlet hawthorn flowers
Flaring and fragrant stand,
Land bird and sea bird bears
Hope of new sea and land'—
If the words are callow
I made them long ago,

But while the wind moves
Behind his hat today
The green glittering leaves,
My father lifts and shows me,
Still usable, though rusted,
The scythe his father lifted,

And like the iron scythe
That hangs out of the rain,
By sharpener and by wrath
Worn down to its backbone,
My life has the shape
That it will keep.

WINTER SEA

I remember, much too early
To see it clearly through the dark lens,
My grandmother among the roses
An old woman with red cheeks—and how she slowly
    built
A ball of silver paper to stand in the never-opened
Dust-proof cabinet below the painting of horses
Running away from lightning.
                               There was a smell
Of coldness in the house and a child could touch
The china jug and basin in the bedroom
Cold and rough to the fingers, or see without stooping
Beyond the verandah a blue cold garden
Through a pane of coloured glass.
                          No doubt her hands were warm.

She carried a sack of oatmeal on her back
Twelve miles, walking beside the breakers
From the town to her own gate. At least once it must
    have happened that a blinding sheet
Of spray rose from the winter waves to cover her.

I go down to the beach and watch the fishermen casting
Their lines out beyond the evening surf.
These men stow tackle in the boots of cars.
Their lead sinkers catch in the crevices of rocks.
No names. No ancestors. The sea stands
Upright like the walls of an empty grave.

THE JAR

Up in Auckland about twelve years ago
In Lowry's house—before the roof fell down
On Lowry's head—I'd bought a peter of wine
From the owner of a Dalmatian vineyard,
And carried it with me wherever I went—
Something to ease the jitters,
Something to have beside my bed in the morning—

And while some were nattering in the kitchen
And some were dancing down on the wooden floor
Of the middle room—half drunk, I held it up,
And saw what I had never even thought of—

On the curve of the wine jar Dionysus lying
Naked and asleep in a black boat,
With a beard like the waves of the sea—and out of his
    belly
A vine growing, vine of ether, vine of earth,
Vine of water—growing towards a sky
Blue as the veins on the inside of a woman's arm—

Black boat, white belly, curved blue sky
Holding us in its hands, as if Earth and Heaven
Wree the friends of man, permanent friends—

A picture of what can't be, as I sat gripped by
The mad, heavy vine of sleep.

INSTRUCTION

The austere angel of the wind
Was our first instructor. He came with a breath of sea-
   weed,
The savour of red currants, or an armful of dry grass,
Blowing our way above gardens and graves.
Drunk with sunlight, we listened
To a monotonous language, not of the ear alone,
Explaining the forms of nature.
                    Either on the wood of the back steps
Where wolf spiders jumped after flies, or under the
   ngaio leaves
Round the corner of the shed. We were children then.
   His voice has changed.
The shed and the house have been pulled down.
I watch the branches of the ngaio tree tremble,
Shaking drops of water onto my coat—
It could be rain; it could be tears—

Those whom I loved as much as I shall ever love
Have joined their voices to that of the wind—
Those whom I loved as much as I shall ever love
Whom the world has turned slowly into air or stone
As I also turn.
               If blood drops rise
To the surface of the grey bark, one should not go
   away.
The words are becoming a little clearer.

THE SAILOR

North of the headland, holding the tiller,
You were aware of islands. Islands
Entering the eye as a burglar enters a room.

The terrible drunkard's longing took hold of you,
To swallow earth, to wrap oneself in leaves,
To stay if necessary ten years on one of those
Bush-covered lozenges of rock,
Beaten by spray, hauling up food in a bucket:

A desire to become luminous
Like stars looked at over hills in the rain.

Later, much later, a glow like fire on the clouds,
It was Auckland breathing in her sleep,
City of wounds, city of friends,
Where one must lift and carry the great boulders.

The dead have now become a part of us,
Speaking between our words, possessing all our dreams.
To be a sailor is to die of thirst.

THE MILLSTONES

I do not expect you to like it. Winter
Has found his way into the tunnels of the mind
And will not leave us.
                  Often between the millstones,
In a stranger's house, perhaps drunk,
One of us would remember
The lagoons and the water birds, sleep that came
Like the travelling of the tide under a boat's keel.

Endlessly in memory I followed the river
To the place it sprang from, among broom bushes
In a gully above the dam. Brother,
It taught me nothing but how to die;
The house is empty. In the paddock alongside it
On a tree, one bitter shrunken apple.
It is the hour of ghosts.
              Do not forget
The time between the millstones was a real time;
The battles were real, foul sweat, foul blood,
Though now the earth is trying to persuade us
We are children again. The gales of the south sea
Will hammer tonight on a shut window.

HERE

Here where the creek runs out between two rocks
And the surf can be heard a mile inland,
And the toetoes hide the nests of a hundred birds,
And the logs lie in the swamp like the bones of giants,
And weed is rotting in heaps on the surface of the
    lagoon,
And the cliff shuts out the sun even at midday,
And the track peters out in banks of seagrass—

Here, where only the wind moves,
I and my crooked shadow
Bring with us briefly the colour of identity and death.

SUMMER 1967

Summer brings out the girls in their green dresses
Whom the foolish might compare to daffodils,
Not seeing how a dead grandmother in each one
   governs her limbs,
Darkening the bright corolla, using her lips to speak
   through,
Or that a silver torque was woven out of
The roots of wet speargrass.
                              The young are mastered by the Dead,
Lacking cunning. But on the beaches, under the clean
   wind
That blows this way from the mountains of Peru,
Drunk with the wind and the silence, not moving an
   inch
As the surf-swimmers mount on yoked waves,
One can begin to shake with laughter,
Becoming oneself a metal Neptune.
                              To want nothing is
The only possible freedom. But I prefer to think of
An afternoon spent drinking rum and cloves
In a little bar, just after the rain had started, in another
   time
Before we began to die—the taste of boredom on the
   tongue
Easily dissolving, and the lights coming on—
With what company? I forget.
                              Where can we find the right
Herbs, drinks, bandages to cover
These lifelong intolerable wounds?
Herbs of oblivion, they lost their power to help us
The day that Aphrodite touched her mouth to ours.

THE GALE

The rubbed unpainted boards of the old church
Catch the sun a little, yawning at death and life
On the ridge below the cabbage tree—and if now the
    heavy wind should blow
Out of the south, scattering thought, making the leaves
    clatter,
I am glad of it.
                    Those who haunt us are useless to us,
And those who haunt us most are the most useless—
The face that wandered in the daytime dream,
The face, the straight brown body and the grip of
    hands,
That fantasy exploded like a light-bulb—
Because the soul by any face is robbed of silence, robbed
    of its own dimension,
Darkness, cold, depth, the cell of storm where now
Out at sea the boats are moving with throbbing engines
Against a proper gale.
                I do not deny these chains
I have to carry; the chains of Eros; but turn to watch
The tide flood in at the river mouth,
Washing under the bridge, making the canoes float
Upside-down.
          Freedom by death is the chosen element.
The black strings of kelp are riding on the tide's cold
    virile breast.

There was a message. I have forgotten it.
There was a journey to make. It did not come to any-
    thing.
But these nights, my friend, under the iron roof
Of this old rabbiters' hut where the traps
Are still hanging up on nails,
Lying in a dry bunk, I feel strangely at ease.
The true dreams, those longed-for strangers,
Begin to come to me through the gates of horn.

I will not explain them. But the city, all that other life
In which we crept sadly like animals
Through thickets of dark thorns, haunted by the
    moisture of women
And the rock of barren friendship, has now another
    shape.
Yes, I thank you. I saw you rise like a Triton,
A great reddish gourd of flesh,
From the sofa at that last party, while your mistress
    smiled
That perfect smile, and shout as if drowning—
'You are always—'
                Despair is the only gift;
When it is shared, it becomes a different thing; like
    rock, like water;
And so you also can share this emptiness with me.

Tears from faces of stone. They are our own tears.
Even if I had forgotten them
The mountain that has taken my being to itself
Would still hang over this hut, with the dead and the
    living
Twined in its crevasses. My door has forgotten how to
    shut.